Rebecca Edwards

Healthy Food...Fast!

Quick, Healthy, Simple Recipes For a Hectic Modern World

Healthy Food..Fast!
Quick, Healthy, Simple Recipes for a Hectic Modern World

Published in the United Kingdom by Onion Custard, Cardiff, UK.
http://publishing.onioncustard.com

Softback Format ISBN: 978-1-909129-60-3

First Edition: October, 2013
Category: Food & Drink / Healthy Eating

Table of Contents

Foreword

I grew up in South Africa and moved to the UK when I was 18 years old. I completed a degree in English and Popular Culture working as a personal trainer and group exercise instructor throughout my studies. It is a career I have pursued ever since.

Having had a great influence from both my parents, I have always taken my diet, health, and training seriously. Both of them are keen cyclists and fantastic cooks. When I lived at home my mother always cooked delicious meals and my father was a wizard in the kitchen. He was always experimenting with different ingredients and bizarre meal ideas. They both love gardening, and grow vegetables and herbs for the family. I believe it was their influence and creativity that stood me in such good stead.

Over the past couple of years I have dedicated myself to learning more and more about nutrition, and I am always looking for and learning new ways to maintain a healthy and enjoyable lifestyle. I look for balance, health and enjoyment and I believe the recipes within my book achieve all three aims.

There is no greater satisfaction than helping clients achieve their goals; watching them adopt a new, healthy lifestyle and seeing the changes occur over the months. It is these people, that I work with every day that make my job so fantastically rewarding and inspiring.

I am just at the start of my journey, but I hope to continue to grow, learn and reap the rewards of my lifestyle choices. I will continue to help people find their balance too. I am so grateful that my passion is my job and that I have the support of like-minded people around me. My partner has been on the receiving end of many of my culinary experiments and I owe him a great deal of thanks for all of his feedback and encouragement. My family have also supported me in everything along the way and for that I am eternally grateful.

Last, but by no means least, I'd like to thank my best friend, Nicola for photographing some of my dishes.

I hope this book gives you what you were looking for, even if you just take one thing away, I hope it is worthwhile in helping you make the changes you need in order to live a healthier lifestyle.

To your continued good health,

Bex

Rebecca Edwards

Introduction

First and foremost I'd like to say thank you for taking the time to purchase this book. I hope that the easy meals and healthy cooking solutions I offer will be a huge help to you. I encourage you to be creative, open-minded and tweak the recipes in places where perhaps they don't suit you. Use this book as a platform to create a healthier lifestyle.

The book is basic, but that is my aim. I want to help to get people back to basics, - back to enjoying healthy fast-food and back to being *human*. Humans were not designed to consume processed food, and I hope this book is a useful tool in getting you back into a more simple way of eating – without compromising on taste or time. I'd like to ensure that it's a lifestyle which is simple to follow. I am a firm believer in having a little bit of what you fancy, and I encourage you to do the same.

Walking the Walk

I live 95% my life eating the recipes in this book. For the other 5% I do enjoy a latte with the girls, or perhaps a glass of wine from time to time. Please bear in mind though that this should all be done within reason, and not to excess.

If you take your training, health and nutrition seriously then everything else will fall into place. Do try to choose your treats and cheats with your health and wellbeing in mind, and indulge a little when your social life suggests it, or perhaps you just fancy an indulgence. Make them an exception, not a habit. Ultimately, live healthy and live happy!

For the last few years, I have endured more 12-15 hour days than I can count. So I know just how it feels to get home and all you want is a quick bite to eat so you can get to bed. That is where this book will help you. It is designed to offer you meal choices based on how much time you are willing to spend in the kitchen – whilst keeping your waistline down and your health in check. My inspiration for this book has come from my determination to lead a healthy lifestyle alongside antisocial working hours.

The Benefits of Healthy Eating

These quick, easy and nutritionally balanced meals will ensure nothing you're eating is processed or ready-made again. Let's start eating food that fits into our hectic lifestyles (and is affordable) without reaching for high fat, high salt, high sugar, or highly processed convenience foods as the solution. Additives, preservatives, colorants, sugars, refined grains and bad fats are all anti-nutrients. Your body has to work hard to digest such things and so by eliminating them you are not asking so much of your body. Following the recipes and advice in this book may lead you to:

- have more energy

- feel more satisfied by what you are eating

- drastically reduce your intake of artificial food additives

- feel healthier

- feel better about your impact on the environment

- taste food differently

- reduce cravings (over time you will not crave fatty, sugary foods as much)

- improve cognitive performance (you may think more clearly)

- lose excess fatty weight

- reduce water retention and bloating

- improve bowel functions and digestion

All of this could add up to a more positive, happier you. Now eating is no longer about surviving, but it is about living.

Let's get back to the healthy stuff because treats shouldn't really be our main focus. Instead, I want to concentrate on the simplicity of maintaining a healthy lifestyle. In keeping with 'going back to basics' I do not intend to sit here and tell you to cook with filtered water, avoid tinned food, and only eat organic fruit and veg or grass-fed free-range meat.

The reality is that many of us think that we can't afford these foods, or that they aren't readily available, or that we simply aren't able to keep it up. If you *can* incorporate these foods into your diet it *will* positively impact your health on an enormous scale so I do strongly recommend adopting them if you can. Evidence shows that in our Western culture we are dangerously unaware of the impact of our food on our lives and its effects on the way we get sick and age. As a nation we are worryingly comfortable with accepting an average state of poor health. We seem to be accustomed to allowing health problems and disease be a part of our everyday life – as if it's inevitable. But by making simple changes to our nutrition, and by factoring good quality food into our daily lives, we *can* dramatically reduce the extent to which many serious diseases develop, and we *can* improve our overall health without medical intervention. Not only that, we can maintain a healthy weight, or lose excess body fat along the way.

I'll leave the organic choices up to you to decide, based on what is best for you, your family and your finances but I will repeat the importance of making such changes *wherever possible.* Local produce need not be expensive or difficult to come by. If you  are buying locally the chances are high that the produce has been picked when ripe, will be fresh and contain more nutrients.

This book is a tool for those seeking simple solutions to a better lifestyle. The meals are nutritionally balanced, fresh and easy to make. Government guidelines defining healthy nutrition are often confusing and vague and I hope this book can offer a little clarity and assist you in giving you ideas in the kitchen.

One of the primary goals of this book is promoting good health. While the adoption of these recipes may result in natural weight loss I come across so many people who are either not over weight, or extremely fit and therefore think that they are healthy and can consume what they like. This couldn't be further from the truth. No matter what your size or fitness level, you should still be making positive choices in terms of your nutrition to ensure you are getting the best for your health and not just watching your waistline.

Fast Food Doesn't Have to Mean Junk Food

The food ideas in this book are based on realistic budgets, realistic time frames and realistic ingredients. I have read plenty of books that, although brilliant, offer recipes with ingredients that are overly expensive, take a long time to prepare, or are difficult to source in the first place.

If a product ends up being a one-off purchase that is unlikely to be used on a regular basis or finished, it's a waste. I'm guilty of losing interest in fancy new foods myself. Although I can be adventurous in the kitchen it tends to be only occasionally, which is great, but for the majority of the time, who am I kidding? I just want to get home, eat quickly, and chill out.

There are numerous diets and healthy eating tips available, and I'm not dismissing all of them out of hand — some do work. It really does depend on your goals though. This book caters for anyone who wants to prepare good food fast and eat healthily and wisely. It's not a panacea for weight-loss.

I advocate reducing our obsession with consuming excessive protein. You cannot make a generic assumption that one diet is going to work for everyone. Personalised consultations are needed. And you need to get to know your own body and your individual needs.

There are plenty of guidelines and dietary advice available, but nobody knows you like you know yourself. Everybody is different and what may work for one person may not work for you. Listen to your body and see what agrees with you. Even food that is widely considered healthy may not be right for you. Become bodily-aware, eat well and eat what works for you.

This is why I have designed a book I feel is as close to catering for the general public as possible. I aimed to make most of the recipes gluten- and dairy-free as such intolerances are common amongst most people today – and many suffer from one or both without even being aware of it. I am not saying every person needs to eliminate dairy or gluten but I do recommend eliminating them, one at a time, on a trial basis if you suspect an intolerance. When you reintroduce them, see how you feel. If you can tolerate them then by all means incorporate small quantities into your diet from time to time.

I promote *sensible* carbs, not cutting them entirely. I haven't overloaded with protein either, but I do offer a balance. And I certainly encourage you to eat an abundance of vegetables.

Variety is the key.

As a nation I feel some of us are guilty of either eating too much (bad quality) meat, too few carbs or the wrong carbs, and definitely not enough fresh produce. Don't get me wrong, meat is hugely nutritional, we are omnivores after all; however with the introduction of diets such as the Paleo or Atkins I think a few things have been lost in translation and the message we've got is to just eat meat. There is far more to it than that and we need to ensure we are getting plenty of goodness from plant sources too. The best way to ensure this is to incorporate more veggie options.

Lastly, do not be afraid of fat. Fat is not your enemy and it is a very important part of our diet. Eating the *right* kind of fat is vitally important to maintain optimal health. Good fats can be found in seeds, nuts, cold-pressed oils, seed oils and olive oil. I have also incorporated coconut oil into many of the recipes. It is a fantastic kitchen essential. Not only does it taste great, making it ideal for baking, but it is also stable at high temperatures making it ideal for frying too. If you cook with olive oil, ensure you do so over a low to medium heat.

I tend to eat veggie 2 - 3 nights a week. Beans and pulses are a fantastic source of fibre and plant protein – and they are cheap. They also provide us with essential nutrients like zinc, folate, iron and magnesium. You may still have a tuna salad or omelette for lunch on a veggie day, but at least by eating veggie for your evening meal, it gives your body a break from too much meat and it's a great way of mixing things up.

My favourite aspect of this is that you get a new feel for flavour. I always find vegetarian food so much more interesting in terms of taste and without the meat you just get a completely different slant on the food. Try it, veggie dishes are tasty, you'll appreciate the difference and will be doing wonders for your health. Nobody, as far as I am aware, has ever suffered from eating too many vegetables! There are plenty of ideas inside so enjoy discovering new flavour combinations.

I have included a lot of the same ingredients across several recipes. There's nothing worse than buying an ingredient and then never using it again. This book will allow you to keep a regular shopping list. By all means experiment, but know that you have a wide selection of nutritious meals you can rely on.

A Bit on the Side

Along with each recipe I have included recommendations of what to have as an accompaniment to the dish. You will also find a section of sides dishes. Many of my clients have said they don't know what to eat other than meat and steamed veg, and that they find it boring. I think this is very often a reason why people don't always succeed with their attempts to eat more healthily.

Use these side dish ideas to accompany any main dish. Remember though, if your main dish is full of ingredients already, often you only need a small helping of steamed veg just to go alongside an already substantial meal. The sides are designed to go alongside a plain or simple main, e.g. with some grilled fish or chicken. You can also bulk up your side dishes and have them as a main meal with a side salad or a bit of veg. Be creative.

One thing to remember on a daily basis – always eat greens. There should always be some kind of green food accompanying your meal, no matter what. They are guilt-free and are great for padding out a dish – plus they have such enormous nutritional value that we need to ensure we are getting plenty of them.

Healthy Snacks

I recommend eating 4-6 small meals a day; in my experience this gives my clients the best results. People tend to forget to snack in between their main meals, or if they do they tend to make bad snack choices – or even worse they binge eat. There are several choices to stick in your lunchbox so you are never caught short on the go. Remember that these are snacks not main meals, so keep the portion sizes small – they should fit easily in your hand.

- Peanut butter bars (pg 91)
- Salsa, guacamole or hummus with vegetable crudités (pg 80)
- Banana and peanut butter
- Boiled eggs
- Oatcakes and salsa
- Oatcakes and peanut butter
- Oatcakes and cottage cheese
- Fruit and yoghurt (pg 90)
- Small handful of nuts
- Berries – blueberries, raspberries, strawberries, etc

The Six Principles of Healthy Food...Fast

#1 Always have something green
      on your plate.

#2 Fill up on vegetables.

#3 Drink 35ml of water per kilo of body weight daily.

#4 Eat veggie twice a week.

#5 Earn your carbs.

Carbs are easily stored as sugar and so eat just enough to maintain energy and sporting performance.

#6 Be Prepared.

If you have a number of business meetings, birthday parties or you're travelling, then you need to be more prepared. Otherwise that 5% treat time will soon become 50%. Enjoy one of those occasions but for the rest of the time you need to be disciplined. Be honest with yourself, be realistic and make healthy choices. Remember, one business buffet does not mean the rest of the day needs to be written off. Be social, eat, enjoy and get straight back to your healthy habits.

Ingredients & Their Health Benefits

I have included a list of the macro-nutrient ingredients you find in foods, and the reasons why they are good for your health. Remember, there are plenty of healthy foods that extend far beyond this list. Make sure your diet is varied and keep on trying new things and eating what is right for *you*.

Although I have placed these ingredients in various food groups they each contain a variety of macro- and micro-nutrients, and categories of food do overlap. Nuts, for example, are not just a source of fat but also a source of protein. These are very general groupings to make things as simple and understandable as possible.

Protein

Proteins function as building blocks for bones, muscles, cartilage, skin, and blood. They are also building blocks for enzymes, hormones, and vitamins. They are essential for our bodies and the key to providing us with enough protein to ensure we are getting a variety of amino acids.

Amino acids are the main constituents of protein, and by giving our body a variety of them we are able to process the essential ones.

Proteins are absolutely vital for growth and maintenance of every kind of cell in our body. Proteins in the form of enzymes, hormones and antibodies promote healthy metabolic and physiological processes, and boost our nervous and immune system. Proteins come in a wide variety of foods.

Animal Protein

• Chicken • Turkey • Beef • Beef • Bacon • Lamb •

Fish

• Tuna • Salmon •

Beans and Pulses

• Chickpeas • Cannelloni Beans • Kidney Beans •
• Butter Beans • White Beans • Lentils •

Fats, Nuts & Oils

Fats are *not* the enemy. They are an integral part of a healthy diet and we most certainly need them. The key is choosing *good* fats.

Saturated fats and trans fats are what we need to stay away from. Bad fats increase cholesterol and your risk of heart disease and diabetes, while good fats protect your heart and support overall health. The healthy fats that you find in all the recipes in this book will play a huge role in helping you manage your moods, improve brain function, fight fatigue, and even control your weight.

On a daily basis we are bombarded with supposedly guilt-free options such as baked products, fat-free ice cream and low-fat sauces These are not really guilt-free and should be avoided at all costs. Is it a coincidence that obesity rates have increased the same time as our nation has become obsessed with eating everything 'low-fat'? I think not. Clearly low-fat foods haven't delivered on their healthy promises.

The answer isn't cutting out fat or reaching for low-fat options; the answer is learning to make healthy fat choices and to replace bad fats with good ones. I even recommend people top up on their fat intake by taking an Omega 3 supplement on a daily basis (seek medical advice before doing so).

The following fats can be found in many of my recipes:

Coconut Oil   Olive Oil
Rapeseed Oil   Olives
Coconut Milk   Nuts
Almonds   Walnuts
Pine Nuts   Tahini
Avocado

19

Carbohydrates

Essentially carbohydrates are our fuel, our energy. For more sustained energy, the aim is to incorporate slow-releasing carbohydrates and thus avoid sudden bursts and peaks and troughs of energy. Fast-release carbs are met by an energy crash on the other side. Instead, we want a slow, steady and consistent release of energy.

Slow-release carbs can be found in fruits, vegetables and wholegrains. The fast energy-releasing carbs to be avoided are found in sugars and refined grains. Slow release carbohydrates can be found in all the foods listed below, along with the many essential micronutrients including phytonutrients and antioxidants they also contain. These additional nutrients are normally absent from refined and processed foods. In addition the foods shown below are also gluten free, which is a lot easier for our bodies to digest.

Seeds and Grains

Quinoa	Bulgar Wheat	Pumpkin Seeds

Fruits and Vegetables

Tomato	Blueberries
Courgettes	Spinach
Banana	Broccoli
Pear	Salad leaves
Mushroom	Pineapple
Sweet Potato	Carrot
Peppers	Cauliflower
Butternut	Onion
Lemons / lemon juice	

Handy Conversion Tables

Weights

Metric	Imperial	Metric	Imperial
15g	½ oz	275g	10 oz
25g	1 oz	300g	11 oz
40g	1½ oz	350g	12 oz
50g	2 oz	375g	13 oz
75g	3 oz	400g	14 oz
100g	3½ oz	425g	15 oz
125g	4 oz	450g	1 lb
150g	5 oz	550g	1¼ lb
175g	6 oz	700g	1½ lb
200g	7 oz	900g	2 lb
225g	8 oz	1.1kg	2½ lb
250g	9 oz		

Volume & Liquids

Metric	Imperial	Metric	Imperial
5ml	1 Teaspoon	200ml	7fl oz
15ml	1 Tablebspoon	250ml	9fl oz
25ml	1fl oz	300ml	½ pint
50ml	2fl oz	500ml	18fl oz
100ml	3½fl oz	600ml	1 pint
125ml	4fl oz	900ml	1½ pints
150ml	5fl oz	1 litre	1¾ pints
175ml	6fl oz		

Cooking Temperatures

Gas Mark	°C	°F
1 – Very Cool	140	275
2	150	300
3	160	325
4	180	350
5	190	375
6	200	400
7	220	425
8	230	450
9 – VERY HOT!	240	475

0.00

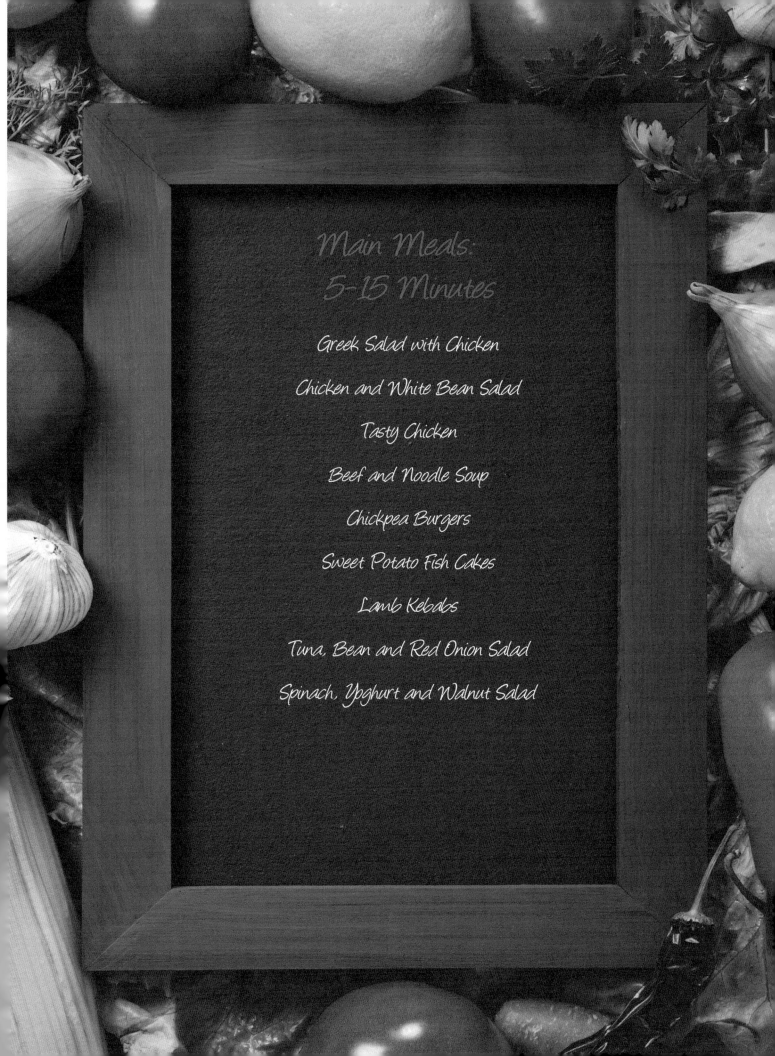

Main Meals:
5-15 Minutes

Greek Salad with Chicken

Chicken and White Bean Salad

Tasty Chicken

Beef and Noodle Soup

Chickpea Burgers

Sweet Potato Fish Cakes

Lamb Kebabs

Tuna, Bean and Red Onion Salad

Spinach, Yoghurt and Walnut Salad

How to Prepare Butternut Squash

Many people shy away from using butternut squash because it can be difficult to peel and buying it ready prepared in a shop is far from ideal. It is very expensive and you only get a very small serving. See below for a quick and easy way of peeling a butternut and start to enjoy using it a lot more in your dishes. It is an excellent source of vitamins A, B6 and C and is also high in fibre and low in calories.

Preparation

Slice through the squash at the narrow neck to separate it from the bottom section then cut off the end from the bottom portion and the top stalk end from the top portion. Next, using a potato peeler, peel the skin from both portions. It is far easier than using a knife and very often when using a knife, you end up losing a lot of the pulp too. Once this has been done, cut each portion of the butternut into rings, scoop out the seeds and stringy pulp along the way.

Sometimes the squash can be difficult and too hard to cut. If this is the case, simply place it in the microwave for 2 -3 minutes (ensure you have poked a few holes in the surface to allow steam to escape) or just until the squash has started to soften. Once the squash is peeled and cut into rings, you can cut it into cubes and begin preparing your dish.

Should you wish to stuff your butternut squash, you needn't bother peeling it. Instead, I would recommend softening it slightly and then cutting it lengthways. Remove all the seeds and stringy pulp as above. Cook as per recipe.

Greek Salad with Chicken

This is quick and easy salad which is light and simple to make. I always keep a few baked chicken breasts in the fridge so that I can make salads like this quickly and without too much fuss.

Time in the Kitchen: 12 mins

Serves 2

Ingredients

250g Chicken Breast
40g Olives
Handful Cherry Tomatoes
40g Cucumber
1 small Onion
40g Low-Fat Feta Cheese
Juice of a Lemon
1 teaspoon Olive Oil

Preparation

✔ Grill the chicken strips until well cooked.
✔ In a bowl, mix together the olives, tomatoes, cucumber, onion and feta cheese.
✔ Squeeze the lemon over the salad and drizzle the olive oil and stir.
✔ Place chicken strips on top of salad and serve.

Chicken & White Bean Salad

I love this salad because it's quick and satisfying. It also keeps well which means you can make a large batch and take it to work with you.

Time in the Kitchen: 15 mins

Serves 4

Mustard Vinaigrette

1 medium clove Garlic, crushed
5 tablespoons Extra-virgin Olive Oil
2 tablespoons Balsamic Vinegar
1 teaspoon Wholegrain Mustard
Pinch of Parsley - preferably fresh
Pinch of Thyme – preferably fresh
2 teaspoon of Lemon Juice
Salt & freshly ground Pepper to taste

Preparation

- ✔ In a small bowl, add the vinegar, garlic & mustard and mix well.
- ✔ Slowly add the olive oil while stirring rapidly with a fork.
- ✔ Add the parsley and lemon juice, thyme, salt and pepper, and season to taste.

Salad

400g tin White Beans, rinsed and drained
600g diced cooked Chicken Breast
100g chopped, Cherry Tomatoes
Salt & freshly ground Pepper to taste (optional)
6 handfuls of a variety of Lettuce, leaves and Spinach
110g finely diced Low-Fat Feta Cheese
300g diced Courgette
1 handful of coarsely chopped fresh Basil

Preparation

✔ Combine beans, chicken, courgette, feta cheese and tomatoes in a large bowl until well blended.
✔ Add chopped basil and ¾ of your already prepared vinaigrette; toss until combined.
✔ Taste and season with salt and pepper, if needed.
✔ Toss the remaining vinaigrette with leaves of your choice in a medium bowl.
✔ Serve the salad on the greens, garnish with fresh basil leaves

Tasty Chicken

Many people get bored with 'diet food' because they think it's all about plain chicken and bland vegetables. Try this dish for something to keep your taste buds excited!.

Time in the Kitchen: 10 mins

Serves 4

Ingredients

1 fresh Red Chilli, deseeded and finely chopped
3 cloves of Garlic, finely chopped
4 Spring Onions, trimmed and finely chopped
1-2 cm piece of Ginger, peeled and ground or cut into wafer thin slices
1 teaspoon ground Coriander
1 teaspoon ground Cumin
4 tablespoons Olive Oil
Salt and Pepper to taste
4 skinless, boneless Chicken Breasts cut into thin slices
1 tablespoon chopped, fresh Coriander

Preparation

✔ Combine the chilli, garlic, spring onions, ginger, ground coriander, cumin, and 3 tablespoons of olive oil in a bowl and season with salt and pepper.
✔ Heat the remaining oil in a wok and add the chicken slices.
✔ Continue to cook for roughly 4 minutes or until the chicken is brown on both sides.
✔ Add the chilli mixture and cook for 4-5 minutes, until the chicken is completely cooked.
✔ Stir in coriander and serve immediately.

Beef and Noodle Soup

Don't be put off by the unusual spices in the soup. The flavours are fantastic and it is so quick and easy.

Time in the Kitchen: 12 mins

Serves 2

Ingredients

1.2 litres of Beef Stock
1 small fresh chopped Chilli
1 Cinnamon Stick
2 Star Anise
2 Cloves
225g Beef Steak, cut into strips
300g Rice Noodles
10 – 15 Broccoli Florets
4 tablespoons chopped, fresh Coriander
Lime wedges to garnish

Preparation

✔ Heat the stock, chilli and spices in a saucepan until boiling, then reduce the heat and simmer for about 5 mins.
✔ Add the beef strips and broccoli and simmer for a further 2-3 mins.
✔ Cook the noodles according to the packet instructions, drain and divide into bowls.
✔ Pour the broth over the noodles
✔ Garnish with coriander and lime and serve.

Chickpea Burgers

Society has become obsessed with 'high protein' diets but the truth is that from time to time is important to mix things up and give your body a meat-free break. Add this great alternative to a burger filled with essential plant protein.

Time in the Kitchen: 12 mins

Serves 4

Ingredients

2 x 400g Chickpeas, drained and rinsed
1 small Onion
Zest and juice of 1 Lime
2 teaspoon ground Coriander
2 teaspoon ground Cumin
6 tablespoons Flour OR 1 Egg
4 tablespoons Olive Oil
4 sprigs of Basil to garnish
Tomato Salsa to serve

Preparation

✔ Put the chickpeas, onion, lime and spices in a food processor and process to a course paste.
✔ Tip the mixture out onto a clean surface and shape in to 4 patties.
✔ If you are having trouble binding add a little whisked egg.
✔ Heat a large frying pan with oil.
✔ Add burgers and cook for 2 mins on each side.

Serving Suggestion

Garnish with basil and serve with salsa/guacamole and a side salad.

Sweet Potato Tuna Cakes

These fish cakes are a great alternative to traditional ones. It is a great low GL (glycaemic loading) dish with lots of essential goodness.

Time in the Kitchen: 15 mins

Serves 2-3

Ingredients

2 large Sweet Potatoes, peeled and chopped
2 x 225g tins of Tuna
2-4 tablespoons Coconut Milk
1 handful of chopped Parsley
1 Egg, beaten
Coconut Oil (If you haven't got any, Olive Oil will do)
Salt and Pepper to taste

Preparation

✔ Put the potatoes into a pan of water and boil until soft.
✔ Meanwhile, place tuna into a mixing bowl along with the parsley. Set to one side.
✔ Once the potatoes are boiled place them in a clean mixing bowl and mash with the coconut milk until you achieve a nice smooth consistency.
✔ Combine the tuna mix with the mashed potato.
✔ Add a little egg. Make sure the mixture isn't too wet, you only need a little egg to help bind the cakes.
✔ Divide the mixture into 4-6 cakes/patties.
✔ Heat the oil in a frying pan and fry the cakes for 5-9 minutes on each side until golden brown.

Lamb Kebabs

These are fun to make and you can add or replace the vegetables with new ones so you have a new dish each and every time.

Time in the Kitchen: 10 mins

Marinade time: ideally 2-3 hours

Serves 4

Marinade

6 tablespoons Olive Oil
Juice of 1 Lemon/4 tablespoons shop-bought Lemon Juice
1 teaspoon mixed Dried Herbs
Soy Sauce to taste
Salt and Pepper to taste

Preparation

✔ Mix all marinade ingredients together and pour over the lamb.
✔ Place in the fridge and allow to marinade for 2 -3 hours.
✔ This will not only flavour the meat but tenderise it too. I try to leave mine overnight for optimum flavour.

Kebabs

500g deboned, cubed Lamb
1 large Onion, cut into large chunks
12-15 Cherry Tomatoes
12-15 small Mushrooms
12 – 15 Pineapple chunks
1 Pepper, cored, seeded and cut into large chunks
8 kebab skewers

Preparation

✔ Once marinated, thread alternative pieces of lamb, onion, tomatoes, mushrooms, pineapple and peppers onto the skewers.
✔ Cook in the oven at 180°C for 10 minutes, or if the weather has been kind, stick them on the BBQ.

Serving Suggestion

Try serving them with the Tzatziki and Grated Carrot Salad.

Tuna, Cannelloni Bean and Red Onion Salad

This is a great one to take into work as it's quick, easy and requires little preparation

Time in the Kitchen: 5 mins

Serves 2

Ingredients

400g Tin of Cannelloni beans, drained and rinsed
1 small Red Onion, finely sliced
1 tablespoon Balsamic Vinegar
1 tablespoon Olive Oil
2 x 225g tins of Tuna
4 tablespoons freshly chopped Parsley
Salt and Pepper to taste

Preparation

✔ Add all of the ingredients in a bowl and mix well.

Serving Suggestion

Serve with a green side salad or a small sweet potato.

Spinach, Yoghurt and Walnut Salad

This salad has great flavours. It is simple, creamy and full of essential fats and important plant nutrients.

Time in the Kitchen: 10 mins

Serves 2

Ingredients

6 Handfuls of fresh Spinach
1 Onion, chopped
1 tablespoon Olive Oil
Salt and Pepper to taste
225 ml Natural Yoghurt
1 Garlic clove, chopped
2 tablespoons chopped Walnuts
2-3 teaspoon chopped fresh Mint

Preparation

- ✔ Fry the onions until soft.
- ✔ Add the spinach and cook gently until wilted.
- ✔ Season with salt and pepper to taste.
- ✔ Combine garlic and yoghurt together in a bowl.
- ✔ Put the spinach and onion in a serving bowl and pour over the yoghurt mixture.
- ✔ Scatter with walnuts and mint.

Serving Suggestion

Serve with a piece of fish, or chicken, and a corn on the cob.

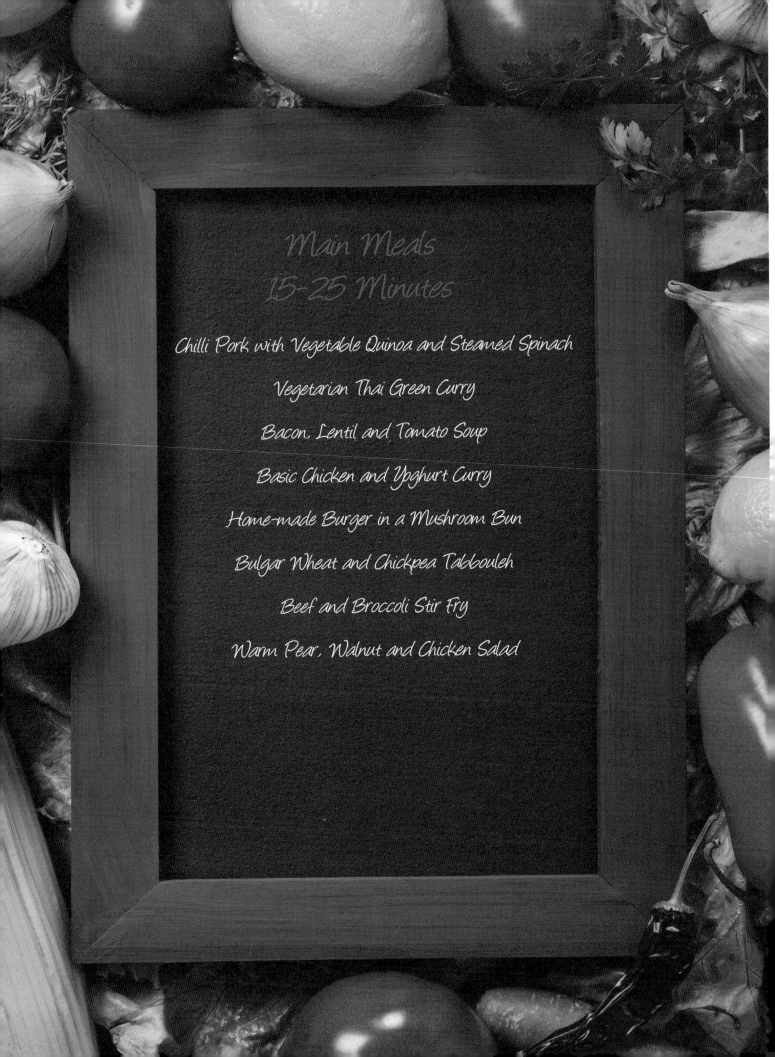

Main Meals
15-25 Minutes

Chilli Pork with Vegetable Quinoa and Steamed Spinach

Vegetarian Thai Green Curry

Bacon, Lentil and Tomato Soup

Basic Chicken and Yoghurt Curry

Home-made Burger in a Mushroom Bun

Bulgar Wheat and Chickpea Tabbouleh

Beef and Broccoli Stir Fry

Warm Pear, Walnut and Chicken Salad

Chilli Pork with Vegetable Quinoa and Steamed Spinach

I love quinoa. It compliments this dish really well with its nutty taste and high protein content.

Time in the Kitchen: 20 mins

Serves 2

Ingredients

1 tablespoon Olive Oil
Juice of 1 Lemon or 4 tablespoons of shop-bought
1 teaspoon Paprika
1 teaspoon Chilli Powder (mild/hot depending on personal preference)
2 Pork medallions, all visible fat removed
100g Quinoa
1 Courgette, finely chopped
1 Red Onion, finely chopped
10-12 Cherry Tomatoes finely chopped
Handful of Flat Leaf Parsley, finely chopped
Handful of Basil, finely chopped
Spinach to serve

Preparation

- ✔ Prepare your Quinoa as per the instructions on the packet.
- ✔ Mix the olive oil, ½ lemon juice, paprika and chilli powder in a ramekin.
- ✔ Brush the mixture over the pork and set to one side.
- ✔ Lightly fry your courgette and onions until both are soft.
- ✔ Set to one side.
- ✔ Heat a frying pan/grill and when it becomes hot, cook your pork medallions on both sides until cooked through. This takes anything from 10 – 12 minutes.
- ✔ While these are cooking, mix all other ingredients and season with salt and pepper. The key to the Quinoa is to use fresh herbs.

Serving Suggestion

Serve Quinoa and Medallions with freshly steamed spinach on the side.

Vegetarian Thai Green Curry

This is a great meat-free alternative which still allows you to enjoy this delicious Thai classic. I often opt for this on a meat-free night. If you're not keen on the veggie option, replace the beans with chicken breast.

Time in the Kitchen: 15-20 minutes

Serves 3-4

Ingredients

1 large Red Onion, sliced
400g tin Butter Beans
2 heaped teaspoon of Thai green curry paste
1 tablespoon Fish Sauce
1 teaspoon grated Ginger
Handful fresh Coriander, chopped

1 teaspoon Olive Oil
400g tin Chick Peas
Juice from 1 Lime

A few Kaffir lime leaves, crushed
1 Garlic Clove, crushed or grated
1 Tin of Coconut Milk

Preparation

✔ Lightly fry the onion in olive oil.
✔ Add the beans and chickpeas along with the curry paste and lightly fry until all the beans are coated.
✔ Add the lime juice and allow to reduce a little.
✔ Add the remaining ingredients, apart from the coconut milk, and allow all the flavours to infuse.

Lastly add the coconut milk and allow to simmer over a low heat while you prepare your cauliflower rice and green beans.

Serving Suggestion

Garnish with leftover fresh coriander.
Serve with lightly steamed fine green beans and cauliflower rice.

Bacon, Lentil and Tomato Soup

This is a delicious winter warmer. Make a large batch and freeze into smaller portions. This way you can take it into work or defrost throughout the day for a quick meal after a long day.

Time in the Kitchen: 15-20 mins

Serves 4

Ingredients

1 tablespoon Olive Oil
2 Onions, peeled and chopped
1 Garlic clove, crushed
2 sticks of Celery
6 rashers of Bacon, chopped with all the fat trimmed off
4 sprigs of Thyme or 2 teaspoon of dried
400g can of Lentils (any type will do)
400g can of chopped Tomatoes (opt for reduced salt where possible)
800 ml Water
2 dried Bay leaves
Bunch of fresh Coriander to serve

Preparation

- ✔ Heat a large saucepan over a medium heat.
- ✔ Add the olive oil and allow to warm through.
- ✔ Add the onions, garlic and celery and cook until soft.
- ✔ Add the bacon and thyme and cook for a further 2 minutes.
- ✔ Drain the water from the lentils and add to the pan along with the tomatoes, water and bay leaves.
- ✔ Increase to a high heat and bring to the boil.
- ✔ Once boiling, reduce the heat and allow to simmer for 15 minutes, stirring occasionally.
- ✔ Once cooked, remove the bay leaves and thyme.

Serving Suggestion

Serve topped with fresh coriander.

Basic Chicken and Yoghurt Curry

I love this recipe because of how simple it is. You can knock this curry up in no time at all and it is really tasty. Very often I have had people tell me they do not enjoy quinoa because it is too bland. The sauce from this curry really jazzes it up so give it a go.

Time in the Kitchen: 15 mins

Serves 2-3

Ingredients

1 tablespoon Olive Oil
1 large Onion, chopped
1 Garlic clove, crushed
1 teaspoon Ginger, minced
2 Chicken Breast fillets
diced Apple (optional)
2 tablespoons Curry powder (medium/hot depending on preference)
1 tablespoon Tomato Purée
5 tablespoons Natural Yoghurt or Fromage Frais
2 tablespoons chopped Almonds
Salt and Pepper to taste

Preparation

- ✔ Heat the oil in a large saucepan over a medium heat.
- ✔ Add the onion and lightly fry until soft.
- ✔ Add the garlic and ginger and fry for a further 2 minutes until the flavours have infused.
- ✔ Now add the chicken and curry powder.
- ✔ Continue to fry and stir all the ingredients so the chicken is well coated.
- ✔ If you like a sweeter curry, now is the time to add the apple to allow it to soften.
- ✔ Add the tomato puree and continue to fry for a further 5 minutes until the chicken is cooked. If you find the pan is starting to become a little dry, add 50 – 100ml of water to allow the chicken to simmer.
- ✔ If you have chosen to add the sweetness of the apple, I would recommend adding the water anyway as it will help in softening the apple.
- ✔ Once the chicken (and apple) is cooked, remove the pan from the heat and slowly add the yoghurt.
- ✔ It is important to do this away from the heat to prevent the yoghurt from curdling.

Serving Suggestion

Add the chopped almonds and serve with quinoa and steamed broccoli and spinach on the side.

Home-made Burger
in a Mushroom Bun

This is a really great low-carb variation of a burger. It's fun to make and a real guilt-free treat.

Time in the Kitchen: 20-25 mins

Serves 4

Ingredients

550g minced Beef or Turkey
25g fresh Coriander, chopped
1 Onion, minced or finely chopped
1 tablespoon Dijon Mustard
1 Garlic clove, minced or finely chopped
1 free-range Egg yolk (if needed)
1 tablespoon Olive Oil
Salt and Pepper to taste
4 x Iceberg Lettuce leaves
8 Portobello Mushrooms
1 Red Onion, sliced
1 Beef Tomato, sliced

Preparation

- ✔ Place all the burger ingredients into a mixing bowl (except for the egg) and using your hands, combine the mixture well. If the mixture feels a little dry, add the egg yolk to ensure the mixture holds together when creating the burger patties.
- ✔ With or without the egg yolk, shape the meat mixture into 4 equal-sized patties.
- ✔ Place in the fridge while you preheat the grill to hot.
- ✔ Once the grill is hot, place the burgers under the grill for 15 minutes or until cooked through, turning once.
- ✔ Just before the burgers are ready, drizzle the mushrooms with a little oil and grill on both sides.
- ✔ When this is done remove the mushrooms from under the grill and top the bottom half of the 'mushroom bun' with a layer of lettuce, sliced tomato and sliced onion.
- ✔ Arrange the burger on top of the layers of veg and finally top with a second mushroom.

Serving Suggestion

Serve with sweet potato chips and a side salad.

Bulgur Wheat and
Chickpea Tabbouleh

This is one of my favourite salads. The flavours work so well together and it always reminds me of the time I spent in the Middle East. I always make a large batch because it keeps really well and is great to take to work. The longer you leave the better the flavours become too. It can be eaten as a large main salad with a small green salad on the side or try it as a side dish with a small piece of chicken or fish.

Time in the Kitchen: 15-20 mins

Serves 2-4

Ingredients

25g Bulgur wheat
1 x 400g tin of Chickpeas
2 large Tomatoes, finely chopped
Large handful of fresh flat-leaf Parsley, finely chopped
Small handful of fresh Mint, finely chopped
1 small Red Onion, finely chopped
3-4 tablespoons freshly squeezed Lemon Juice
4-5 tablespoons Extra Virgin Olive Oil
Salt and Pepper to taste
1 teaspoon Chilli flakes (optional)

Preparation

- ✔ Bring a small pan of water to the boil.
- ✔ Reduce the heat and add the bulgur wheat. Leave for 10 – 15 minutes until cooked through, keep an eye on it and stir occasionally.
- ✔ Meanwhile, place the tomatoes, parsley, mint, onion and tomatoes into a bowl and mix well until combined.
- ✔ If using tinned chickpeas, drain the water. Add the chickpeas to the bowl too.
- ✔ Once the bulgur wheat is cooked, drain any water which hasn't been absorbed, fluff up the bulgur wheat and add to the chickpea and tomato mix.
- ✔ Drizzle the salad with lemon juice and olive oil and season to taste.
- ✔ Mix well to coat all the ingredients and serve.

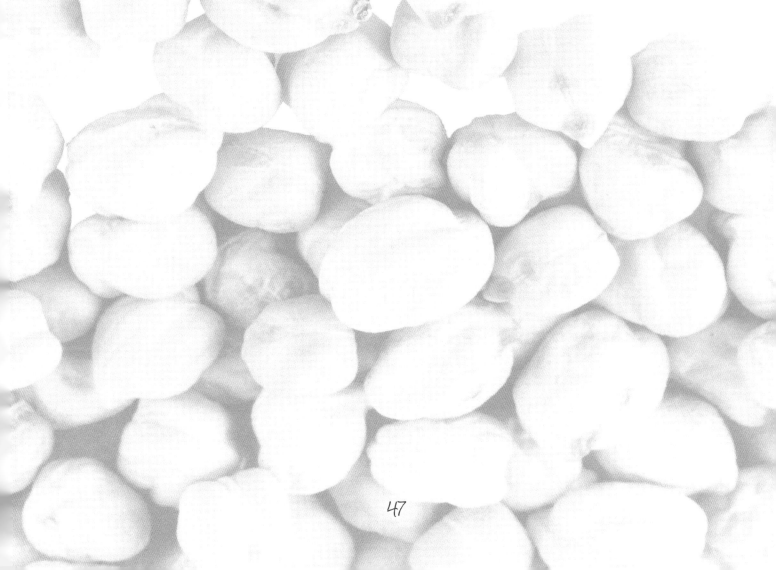

Beef and Broccoli Stir-fry

This is simple, low carb and really tasty.... Enjoy! If you were after a meal with a few more carbs, try adding a side of sweet potato mash. The flavours complement each other really well.

Time in the Kitchen: 15-20 mins

Serves 3-4

Ingredients

450g Frying Steak
3 tablespoons Soy Sauce
1 tablespoon Sesame Oil
1 teaspoon Chinese Five Spice
2 teaspoon Ginger, grated
1 Garlic clove, crushed
1 large head of Broccoli, cut into florets
170g Bean Sprouts
1 handful fresh Mint, chopped
1 handful fresh Coriander, chopped

Preparation

- ✔ Begin by lightly steaming your broccoli. Ensure the broccoli is 'al dente' - ensure it is cooked to a tender-crisp. This takes roughly 3 – 5 minutes.
- ✔ Meanwhile, mix together the soy sauce, sesame oil, Chinese five spice, ginger and garlic to create a marinade for the meat.
- ✔ Slice your steaks into thin strips and coat in the marinade.
- ✔ If you have time, leave to marinade for a few hours, the longer the better. However, if your time is limited, leave to marinade for a minimum of 15 minutes.
- ✔ Once your meat is marinated, heat a sauté pan or wok, add the meat and sauté for 3-5 minutes.
- ✔ Add the broccoli and sauté for a further 2 -3 minutes.
- ✔ Add the beans sprouts and remove from heat.

Serving Suggestion

Garnish with fresh herbs and serve.

Warm Pear, Walnut and Chicken Salad

The sweetness of the pear combined with the crunchy walnuts and succulent chicken makes this salad a must. It is a delicious balance of carbohydrates, fats and protein and just another simple way of enjoying good food.

Time in the Kitchen: 20-25 mins

Serves 3-4

Ingredients

2 Chicken Breast Fillets
2 medium sized Pears
40g chopped Walnuts
1 tablespoon walnut oil
   (If you haven't got walnut oil, any other nut oil or olive oil will do)
1 tablespoon butter
60g Mixed Salad leaves
Balsamic Glaze (optional)

Preparation

- ✔ Preheat the oven to 180°C and place chicken breast in the oven to bake for 20 – 25 minutes.
- ✔ Meanwhile, cut the pears lengthways into quarters, remove the cores but leave the skins on. Then, cut each quarter into 4 slices.
- ✔ Heat the walnut oil in a large frying pan over a medium heat and lightly fry the walnuts.
- ✔ Keep the walnuts moving in the pan, tossing them around for about 1 minute.
- ✔ Once this has been done, remove the walnuts from the pan and place to one side on a plate.
- ✔ Using the same frying pan, melt the butter over a medium heat and lightly fry the pears until brown on each side.
- ✔ Set to one side but ensure you keep the pears warm.
- ✔ Once the chicken breast is cooked through, remove from the oven and cut into small slices.
- ✔ Place the lettuce leaves in a medium sized salad bowl and add the pears, chicken and walnuts.
- ✔ Toss the leaves to ensure all the ingredients are well combined.

Serving Suggestion

Serve and dress with a little balsamic glaze if desired.

Main Meals
25-50 Minutes

Turkey and Rocket Kofta

Sweet Potato Mini Frittatas

Roasted Red Pepper and Onion Soup

Lentil Chilli with Cauliflower Rice

Cumin Salmon with Sweet Potato Wedges
and Steamed Green Veg

Turkey Bacon and Lentil Stuffed Peppers

Chickpea and Butternut Squash

Quinoa Stuffed Butternut Squash

Warm Lentil, Sweet Potato, Chicken and Broccoli Salad

Sweet Potato, Chicken and Honey Mustard Salad

Pesto Stuffed Chicken Breast

Sweet Potato, Spinach and Turkey Mince Cottage Pie

Lemony Spinach Soup

Honey and Citrus Chicken

Turkey and Rocket Kofta

Kofta are oval shaped meatballs from the Middle East and are usually made from minced lamb or beef but this turkey recipe is just as delicious and is much lower in fat. The rocket adds an interesting peppery twist and keeps it nice and light.

Time in the Kitchen: 25-30 mins

Serves 3-4

Ingredients

400g lean Turkey Mince
50g Rocket, finely chopped
half cup cooked Couscous
2 cloves of Garlic, minced or finely chopped
half teaspoon Paprika
1 Egg, beaten
Salt and Pepper to taste
Half a Lemon

Preparation

✔ Preheat the oven to 180°C.
✔ Line an oven tray with baking paper.
✔ Combine all the ingredients in a large bowl and mix well.
✔ Using your hands shape the meat mixture into 8 small oval shaped patties and place on the oven tray.
✔ Refrigerate for 10 minutes.
✔ Bake for 15 – 20 minutes until cooked through.

Serving Suggestion

Serve with a mixed bean salad and some extra rocket on the side.

Sweet Potato Mini Frittatas

This recipe is great to take to work for a snack/ lunch if you have any leftovers.

Time in the Kitchen: 35 mins

Makes 12 Muffin-Sized Frittatas.

Ingredients

Olive Oil Spray
250g Sweet Potato, peeled and chopped into 1cm cubes
6 Eggs, beaten
75ml Milk
225g tin Tuna
Handful of Spinach
1 tablespoon fresh Chives, finely chopped
90g Low-Fat Feta Cheese, crumbled
Salt and freshly ground black Pepper to taste
You will also need a 12-hole muffin tin and
   non-stick baking paper.

Preparation

- ✔ Preheat oven to 200° C. Spray a 12-hole muffin tin with olive oil spray and set to one side. Cut 12 x 15 cm squares of non-stick baking paper and place one in each hole of the muffin tin.
- ✔ Once the tins are lined, line the paper with a few spinach leaves to create a base for your egg mixture.
- ✔ In a pan of boiling water, cook the sweet potato for 5 minutes until tender. Drain and leave to cool.
- ✔ In a large mixing bowl, combine the eggs, milk, tuna, chives and feta and season well.
- ✔ Divide the sweet potato cubes evenly between the muffin holes and the spoon over the egg mixture. Bakes for 18 – 20 minutes or until golden and the eggs are set.
- ✔ Remove from oven and allow to cool for 5 minutes.

Serving Suggestion

Serve with a fresh side salad or steamed green veg.

Roasted Red Pepper
and Onion Soup

This is a great recipe for when you are already in the kitchen. There is limited preparation and you can stick everything in the oven whilst cooking another meal. It is a great way to get organised and prepare your lunch for work the next day or stick it in the freezer to save yourself some time in the future.

Time in the Kitchen: 45 mins

Serves 2-3

Ingredients

2 teaspoon Olive Oil
1 Red Pepper
1 Yellow Pepper
1 Orange Pepper
2 handfuls of Cherry Tomatoes
1 Red Onion
1 teaspoon Dried Rosemary Needles/4 – 5 sprigs of fresh
300ml Vegetable Stock

Preparation

- ✔ Preheat oven to 200°C.
- ✔ Drizzle the olive oil into a roasting tray.
- ✔ Add the peppers, tomatoes and onions and toss them in the oil to coat them.
- ✔ Add the rosemary and roast for 40 minutes until tender.
- ✔ Transfer the roasted vegetables (remove rosemary if you used fresh) and stock, to a blender or food processor and blend until smooth.
- ✔ Transfer to a saucepan and heat over on a low heat for 2 minutes until piping hot.
- ✔ Season and serve.

Lentil Chilli with Cauliflower Rice

Another meat-free alternative to a family favourite. The beans work so well with the flavours of a traditional chilli. I made this at a yoga retreat I catered for and it was a hit.

Time in the Kitchen: 30 mins

Serves 2-3

Ingredients

1 tablespoon Olive Oil
1 Onion
1 Garlic clove, crushed
Salt and Pepper
1 teaspoon dried Chilli Flakes
1 teaspoon Chilli Powder (Medium/Hot depending on personal preference)
1 teaspoon Paprika
1 teaspoon ground Cumin
1 teaspoon dried Oregano
400g tin Chopped Tomatoes
2 tablespoons Tomato Purée
400g tin Red Kidney Beans
400g tin Lentils (Puy Lentils ideally but Green Lentils are just as nice)
1 large Cauliflower for 'Rice' (see Cauliflower Rice recipe)
Green Veg of your choice to serve with the meal

Preparation

- ✔ Heat the oil in a large saucepan. Add the onion and cook for 5 minutes. Add the garlic and salt and pepper and cook for a further 1 minute.
- ✔ Add the spices and tinned tomatoes to the pan and allow to simmer for 10 minutes. Add the tomato puree, kidney beans and lentils and allow to simmer for a further 10 minutes.
- ✔ Meanwhile, prepare your cauliflower rice (recipe available on page.....). Steam your green veg and serve.
- ✔ *Note* The longer you leave your chilli to stew, the better the taste. I usually make mine the day before. The flavours are great.

Cumin Salmon with Sweet Potato Wedges and Steamed Green Veg

The spices used to coat the fish create a really tasty flavour. For a quicker meal, replace the sweet potato with some added steamed veg.

Time in the Kitchen: 45–50 mins

Serves 2

Ingredients

500g Sweet Potatoes
2 tablespoons Olive Oil/Rapeseed Oil
4 sprigs of Rosemary, leaves removed and finely chopped or 1 tablespoons of dried Rosemary
1 Garlic clove, crushed
2 x 125g fresh Salmon Fillet
1 teaspoon ground Cumin
1 teaspoon Chilli powder (medium/hot depending on personal preference)
1 teaspoon Paprika
Freshly ground Black Pepper
Green Vegetable to serve

Preparation

✔ Preheat oven to 180°C. Scrub the sweet potatoes and then slice into wedges. Tip into a large plastic food bag along with oil, garlic and rosemary. Seal the bag and rub to ensure the potatoes are evenly coated. Tip the wedges onto a baking sheet and roast for 45 minutes or until tender.

✔ While wedges are cooking, place foil on a baking tray and lightly spray with oil. Combine all the remaining spices in a small ramekin.

✔ Rinse fish and pat dry. Place fish, skin side down, on the baking tray and sprinkle with your spices.

✔ 12 minutes before the potatoes have finished roasting, place the salmon on the middle shelf in the oven and bake for 12 minutes.

✔ During this time, lightly steam your choice of green vegetables. Serve

Turkey Bacon and Lentil Stuffed Peppers

Bacon is great for an occasional treat and to add variety to your dishes. This is really delicious and looks lovely when served. It's a great one to make before-hand and then bake when ready.

For an added twist, crumble some feta cheese onto the peppers just before sticking them in the oven.

Time in the Kitchen: 25-35 mins

Serves 2

(with some lentil mix left over for lunch the next day)

Ingredients

2 x Peppers
1 x small Red Onion
2 cloves of Garlic
6 -8 rashers of Turkey Bacon, chopped
1 teaspoon Cumin
1 teaspoon Chilli powder (mild/hot depending on personal preference)
400g tin chopped Tomatoes
1 teaspoon Oregano (fresh is best but dry is just as good)
100g Bulgur wheat/Quinoa (Cooked)
100g Lentils, cooked(I use Puy lentils but any type will do)
Green veg of your choice to serve

Preparation

- ✔ Preheat oven to 180°C.
- ✔ Lightly fry the onions and garlic until onions are soft.
- ✔ Add the turkey bacon and continue to fry until cooked.
- ✔ Add the cumin and chilli powder and cook for a further 2 minutes.
- ✔ When all ingredients are golden brown, add your tin of tomatoes and oregano and allow to simmer for 15 minutes.
- ✔ Then add your bulgur wheat/quinoa and lentils.
- ✔ Stir well and leave to simmer whilst you prepare your peppers.
- ✔ De-seed peppers and cut in half length way.
- ✔ Scoop 2-3 tablespoons of your mix into each pepper.
- ✔ Bake in the oven for 18 – 20 minutes.
- ✔ I prefer my pepper al dente however you can leave them in a little longer if you prefer them softer.

Serving Suggestion

Serve with fresh, steamed green veg of your choice or a side salad.

Chickpea and Butternut Squash

Some good quality plant protein and essential fats too. Enjoy this recipe packed full of superfood ingredients.

Time in the Kitchen: 25 mins

Serves 4

Ingredients

900g Butternut Squash, peeled and seeded and cubed into 2cm pieces
1 Garlic clove, crushed
2 tablespoons Olive Oil
2 x 400g Chickpeas
1 Red Onion, thinly sliced
1 large bunch of Coriander, roughly chopped
Salt and Pepper to taste
Tahini Sauce: (is this a sub head)
3 tablespoons Tahini Paste
1 Garlic clove, crushed
Juice of 1 Lemon or 4 tablespoons of shop-bought

Preparation

- ✔ Preheat the oven to 220°C.
- ✔ Toss the butternut in the oil and garlic and season.
- ✔ Place in a roasting dish and roast for 20 minutes or until soft.
- ✔ While the butternut is in the oven, begin to prepare the remaining ingredients.
- ✔ Place the chickpeas in a pan and cover with water. Warm over a medium heat.
- ✔ To prepare the tahini sauce, place the garlic and some seasoning in a bowl, then whisk in the tahini paste.
- ✔ Add the lemon juice plus 4-5 tablespoons of water so that you create a creamy consistency.
- ✔ Drain the chickpeas, put in a large bowl and place in a mixing bowl, then add the butternut squash, onion and coriander.
- ✔ Pour over the tahini sauce and lightly toss.

Serving Suggestion

Serve as a main dish with some spinach and broccoli on the side or as a side dish with a chicken breast and green veg.

Quinoa Stuffed Butternut Squash

This is a great vegetarian dish with lots of delicious flavours. If you'd like to add meat to the dish, bake a chicken breast and have half the butternut portion along with some steamed green veg.

Time in the Kitchen: 45-60 mins

Serves 2-4

Ingredients

1 medium Butternut Squash
2 tablespoons Olive Oil, for roasting
1 Garlic clove, crushed
150g Quinoa
50g toasted Pine Nuts
1 small Carrot, grated
Small bunch Chives, snipped
Juice of half a Lemon
1 Red Pepper, chopped
Handful of Cherry Tomatoes, chopped in half
50g pitted Black Olives
2 Spring Onions, chopped
80g Feta Cheese
Salt and Pepper to taste

Preparation

- ✔ Heat the oven to 200°C.
- ✔ Halve the butternut squash (as per instruction on page.......).
- ✔ Arrange the two halves on a baking tray.
- ✔ In a small dish, mix the garlic with the olive oil.
- ✔ Drizzle the olive oil and garlic mixture over the butternut, season with freshly ground black pepper and sea salt and cook for 40 - 50 minutes until soft.
- ✔ Meanwhile bring a pan of water to boil and cook quinoa as per manufacturer's instructions.
- ✔ Drain any remaining water and set aside to cool once cooked. In a small frying pan, dry fry the pine nuts for 2 -3 minutes then add the remaining ingredients (except for the feta cheese) and fry until cooked.
- ✔ Add any remaining garlic oil if required.
- ✔ Combine the fried ingredients with the cooked quinoa and feta cheese, mix well and set to one side.
- ✔ Once the butternut is done, take out the oven and stuff with the quinoa mix by spooning the filling into the butternut squash.
- ✔ Return to the oven for a further 10 mins.

Serving Suggestion

Serve with lightly steamed green vegetables. Spinach complements this dish really well.

Warm Lentil, Sweet Potato, Chicken, and Broccoli Salad

Salads do not need to be boring or bland... try this recipe!

Time in the Kitchen: 25-35 mins

Serves 4

Ingredients

2 large Sweet Potatoes, peeled and chopped into 2 cm cubes
2 tablespoons Olive Oil
350g Chicken Breast
125g Lentils (Puy are best but green will do)
1 large Garlic clove, crushed
1 teaspoon Salt
1 teaspoon English Mustard Powder
2 tablespoons Balsamic Vinegar
4 tablespoons Rapeseed Oil
1 Red Onion, thinly sliced
Salt and Pepper to taste

Preparation

- ✔ Preheat the oven to 220°C.
- ✔ Toss the sweet potato in the olive oil and season.
- ✔ Place in a roasting dish and roast for 20 minutes or until soft.
- ✔ In a separate dish, place the chicken breast in the oven too and bake until cooked through.
- ✔ The chicken and potatoes will be ready at the same time.
- ✔ Meanwhile, if using raw lentils, cook in unsalted water for 35 minutes until soft.
- ✔ If using tinned lentils, heat them up in a saucepan.
- ✔ Meanwhile, lightly steam the broccoli, ensuring it remains tender.
- ✔ Combine the garlic and salt in a bowl. Add the mustard powder and mix well. Add the vinegar and 3tablespoons of rapeseed oil and set to one side.
- ✔ Remove the chicken and sweet potato from the oven. Cut the chicken into strips.
- ✔ Add the remaining rapeseed oil into a frying pan and lightly fry the onion.
- ✔ Once the onions have begun to soften, add the chicken, broccoli and sweet potato and lightly stir-fry for 1-2 minutes.
- ✔ Drain the lentils and combine with the broccoli mix in a large bowl.
- ✔ Stir the dressing through the mixture. Season and serve warm.

Sweet Potato, Chicken, and Honey Mustard Salad

Another super salad to add variety to your healthy lifestyle. It is simple and very tasty.

Time in the Kitchen: 20-25 mins

Serves: 4

Ingredients

3 tablespoons Coconut Oil
1 Garlic clove, crushed
2 medium Sweet Potatoes, peeled and diced
300g Chicken Breast, cut into strips
1 teaspoon Garlic Powder
1 teaspoon Cayenne Pepper
Salt and Pepper to taste
Half a Cucumber, diced
1 small Red Onion, diced
4 tablespoons Dijon Mustard
3 tablespoons Honey

Preparation

- ✔ Begin by lightly boiling the sweet potato chunks until slightly soft.
- ✔ Meanwhile, place the coconut oil and garlic into a frying pan placed over a medium heat and allow the garlic to become fragrant.
- ✔ Add the chicken and lightly fry until cooked.
- ✔ Drain the boiling water from the potatoes and then add the lightly boiled potatoes to the chicken mixture.
- ✔ Season the chicken and sweet potato with the garlic powder, cayenne pepper and salt and pepper.
- ✔ Cook for a further 2 minutes and then set to one side.
- ✔ Add the red onion and cucumber to a large salad bowl, along with the honey and mustard.
- ✔ Once you have done this, add the chicken and potato mixture to the salad bowl and mix thoroughly.

Serving Suggestion

Serve with a handful of rocket.

Pesto-Stuffed Chicken Breast

Who needs pasta to accompany pesto? This is one of my favourite recipes and gives the chicken a delicious flavour. If you make a large batch of pesto, you can freeze it and use it again to save yourself time.

Time in the Kitchen: 30-35 mins

Serves 3

Ingredients

100g Pine Nuts
20g Basil
1 Garlic clove
125ml Olive Oil
1 tablespoon Lemon Juice
Salt and Pepper to taste
3 x Chicken Breast fillets
Kebab sticks/Toothpicks

Making the Pesto

- ✔ Put pine nuts in a dry heavy-bottomed frying pan and cook for 3 minutes.
- ✔ Stir frequently until golden.
- ✔ Transfer pine nuts into a blender and add the basil leaves, garlic clove, olive oil, lemon juice and salt and pepper.
- ✔ Blend for 35 seconds, or until well combined

Preparing the Chicken Breast

✔ Butterfly your chicken breasts.
✔ Turn the breast over on its thinner edge and, with the edge of a knife parallel to the cutting board, begin cutting down the length of the side of the breast.
✔ Carefully slice the breast in half width wise almost to the other edge. Keep that edge intact and open the breast along the "fold".
✔ Take your freshly prepared pesto and place 1 teaspoon of pesto/per chicken breast and spread evenly along the inside breast.
✔ Fold the chicken breast back over and secure with toothpicks or kebab skewers.
✔ Bake in the oven for 25–30 minutes at 180C.
✔ Meanwhile prepare a fresh salad.
✔ Once chicken is thoroughly cooked, serve with your salad and enjoy.

Sweet Potato, Spinach and Turkey Mince Cottage Pie

This recipe is worth making just for the pretty colours but it is full of healthy ingredients too. It is a great one as you can freeze it so you've always got a healthy meal at hand.

Time in the Kitchen: 60 mins

Serves 4

Ingredients

1 tablespoons Oil
1 large Onion, chopped
1 Garlic clove, minced or finely chopped
2 medium Carrots, chopped
500g Turkey mince
1 x 400g tin of chopped Tomatoes
2 tablespoons Tomato purée
300ml Vegetable Stock
1 cup frozen Peas
1 teaspoon Dried Mixed Herbs
Dash of Worcestershire sauce
1 kg Sweet Potato, peeled and diced
2 teaspoon Dijon Mustard
2 cups frozen Spinach, defrosted

Preparation

- ✔ Preheat the oven to 190°C.
- ✔ Heat the oil in a large frying pan over a medium – high heat.
- ✔ Add the onion, garlic and carrot and lightly fry until soft.
- ✔ Add the mice and cook for a further 5 minutes.
- ✔ Add the tinned tomatoes, tomato purée, vegetable stock, frozen peas, mixed herbs and Worcestershire sauce.
- ✔ Season with salt and pepper to taste, cover and allow to simmer for 20 minutes.
- ✔ Meanwhile, boil the sweet potatoes until soft. Drain and mash until smooth.
- ✔ Combine the sweet potato mash with the mustard and the spinach.
- ✔ Season with salt and pepper to taste.
- ✔ Spoon the mince mixture into a medium-sized oven-proof dish and top with sweet potato and spinach mixture.
- ✔ Bake for 25–30 minutes until golden brown.

Serving Suggestion

Serve with some lightly steamed green veg or a fresh side salad

Lemony Spinach Soup

This is a great winter warmer with a hearty helping of healthy stodge to keep you going all day.

Time in the Kitchen: 30-35 mins

Serves 2

Ingredients

250g of a mixture of your favourite Beans, Pulses and Grains
  (my favourite mixture is quinoa, lentils, bulgur wheat and kidney beans)
1 tablespoon Olive Oil
1 Onion, finely chopped
1 Garlic clove, minced or
  finely chopped
1 Vegetable Stock cube
1 Star Anise
1 litre of Water
250g fresh Spinach
3 tablespoons Lemon Juice
Salt and Pepper to taste

Preparation

- ✔ Heat the oil in a small saucepan.
- ✔ Add the onion and garlic and cook until soft. Set aside.
- ✔ Meanwhile, put your choice of beans, pulses and grains into a heavy based saucepan.
- ✔ Crumble the stock cube into the mix and stir until coated.
- ✔ Add the star anise and water.
- ✔ Bring to the boil, then reduce the heat and simmer for 5 minutes.
- ✔ Add the spinach. When wilted, add the onion and garlic mix, then the lemon juice. Season to taste, serve and enjoy.

Honey and Citrus Chicken

As I have said time and time again, healthy food is not just a case of bland meat and vegetables. These flavours complement the chicken really well and are a great way of jazzing up a chicken breast.

Time in the Kitchen: 35 mins

Serves 4

Ingredients

4 teaspoon Honey
4 Chicken Breasts
Juice of 1 Orange or 10 tablespoons of shop-bought
Juice of a Lemon or 4 tablespoons of shop-bought
1 tablespoon Soy Sauce
Salt and Pepper to taste

Preparation

- ✔ Preheat oven to 180°C.
- ✔ Place chicken breast in a shallow baking dish.
- ✔ Rub a teaspoon of honey into each chicken breast.
- ✔ In a separate small dish, mix together the remaining ingredients and pour over the chicken.
- ✔ Cover the dish with foil and bake for 30 minutes or until the chicken is cooked through.
- ✔ Take the foil off for the last 5 of minutes and spoon any liquid in the pan, over the chicken breasts. This will ensure they remain moist.

Sides, Dips and Sauces

Cannelloni Bean Mash

Guacamole

Tzatziki

Funky Sweet Potato

Yoghurt Marinade

Spicy Cajun Marinade

Spicy Chickpeas with Tomato

Hummus

Griddled Courgettes with Feta, Lemon, Mint and Lentils

Grated Carrot Side Salad

Cauliflower Rice

Cannelloni Bean Mash

For a great alternative to a carb-heavy mashed potato, why not try this recipe. It goes well with some green beans and a piece of tuna or even with some low-fat turkey sausages and home-made gravy.

Time in the Kitchen: 7 mins

Serves 3-4

Ingredients

2 x 400g cans of Cannelloni Beans, drained
1 tablespoon Olive Oil
4 tablespoons Low-Fat Natural/Greek Yoghurt
1 Garlic clove, crushed
Salt and Pepper

Preparation

✔ Heat ingredients in a saucepan until bubbling, season with salt and pepper to preferred taste.
✔ Mash and serve.

Guacamole

A classic, and a great source of essential fat. It is perfect to eat with some vegetable crudités or oatcakes for a nutritious snack.

Time in the Kitchen: 15 mins

Serves 3-4

Ingredients

2 cloves of Garlic, crushed
½ Red Onion finely chopped. The smaller the pieces the better
2 small Red Chillies/1 tablespoons Dried Chilli flakes (adjust according to personal taste)
5-6 ripe Avocados, peeled with stone removed
2 large ripe Tomatoes, very finely diced
Juice of 2-4 Limes (This is just to stop the avocado going brown so taste as you add)
A couple of drops of Chilli Sauce, to taste
Salt and Pepper, to taste
Handful of freshly chopped Coriander

Preparation

✔ Combine the garlic, onion and chillies in a bowl.
✔ In a separate dish, mash the avocado into a paste. Some prefer to leave it a little chunky, this is down to personal preference.
✔ Now combine all the ingredients together in one dish.
✔ Go easy on the lime juice.

Serving Suggestion

Serve with a cold chicken salad or for a great snack, spread onto some oat cakes, rice cakes or even a Ryvita.

Tzatziki

Another delicious dip to have with oat cakes or crudités so that your diet never gets boring.

Time in the Kitchen: 10 mins

Serves 4

Ingredients

125g Low-Fat Greek Yoghurt
1 Garlic clove, crushed
1 small handful of Chives, chopped
1 small handful of Mint, chopped
1 medium Cucumber, peeled and finely diced

Preparation

✔ Mixed all ingredients together and serve.

Serving Suggestion

Ideal with a grilled chicken breast and a small side salad. Alternatively use a dip with oatcakes, rice cakes, Ryvita® or some carrot sticks.

Yoghurt Marinade

Simple, low-fat and another way of trying something different with your meat.

Time in the Kitchen: 10 mins

Serves 3-4

Ingredients

500g Natural Yoghurt
2 handfuls of fresh Mint
Grated zest and juice of 2 Limes or 4 tablespoons Lime Juice
1 tablespoon Coriander (ideally fresh but dry will do)
1 teaspoon Olive Oil
Salt and Pepper to taste

Preparation

- ✔ Place all ingredients in a bowl and mix together.
- ✔ Cover any type of white meat or fish with marinade and allow to marinade for 30 minutes at the very least. Ideally leave to marinade for 4-6 hours.
- ✔ Cook meat according to requirements and serve with fresh veg.

Spicy Cajun Marinade

A great marinade for BBQ. Herbs and spices are a fantastically healthy way of adding flavour to your food.

Time in the Kitchen: 10 mins

Serves 2-3

Ingredients

2 tablespoons Paprika
2 tablespoons Cayenne Pepper
1 clove Garlic, crushed
1 small Onion, minced or very finely chopped
2 tablespoons Dried Oregano

Preparation

Pound all ingredients together. Rub all over any meat of your choice. Allow to marinade for at least 30 minutes before cooking.

Personally I enjoy this marinade with a piece of steak, grilled and served with a rocket salad in the summer or some lightly steamed broccoli in the winter.

Spicy Chickpeas with Tomato

A favourite with all my clients and a great source of plant protein and fibre. I enjoy this cold as a snack too.

Time in the Kitchen: 15 mins

Serves 2-3

Ingredients

1 teaspoon Olive Oil
1 Onion, chopped
1 teaspoon, Ground Cumin
1 teaspoon, Ground Coriander
1 teaspoon, Ground Turmeric
1 small Red Chilli, finely chopped
1 x 400g can Chickpeas, rinsed and drained
250g Cherry Tomatoes
¼ cup Chopped Coriander leaves

Preparation

✔ Heat the oil in a saucepan over a medium heat.
✔ Cook the onion for 5 minutes or until tender.
✔ Add the spices and chilli and cook for 1 minute.
✔ Add the chickpeas and cook over a low heat for 6 minutes.
✔ Stir in the tomatoes and coriander and simmer for 3 minutes.

Serving Suggestion

Serve this as a main meal for 1 with a small rocket salad on the side. If serving as a side dish, try it with a baked chicken and hearty helping of spinach.

Hummus

This is a great dip. Grab yourself some cucumber and carrot sticks for a simple nutritious on-the-go snack. Don't let it seem like a hassle to make. Make yourself a large batch and leave it in the fridge. It is also delicious with oatcakes. Almost all shop-bought hummus is scarily high in salt. Also use as a healthy alternative to mayonnaise.

Time in the Kitchen: 10 mins

Serves 4-6

Ingredients

180g Chickpeas (tinned are fine, keep back a little of the water)
Juice of 2 Lemons/4 tablespoons Lemon Juice
2 cloves of Garlic, crushed
4 tablespoons Tahini
   (available in most supermarkets and definitely in health food stores)
2 tablespoons Olive Oil (optional)

Preparation

- ✔ Drain chickpeas ensuring to save a little water.
- ✔ Blend in a food processor.
- ✔ Add the remaining ingredients (except for the oil) and blend for a further 2 minutes until smooth.
- ✔ Add 2 tablespoons oil and blend to an even smoother paste.
- ✔ For a low- fat option, use the chickpea water instead.
- ✔ Taste and adjust seasoning accordingly.

Griddled Courgettes with Feta, Lemon, Mint and Lentils

Not only does this taste great but it looks great too. It makes for a lovely light lunch and is one to consider if you are entertaining.

Time in the Kitchen: 30-35 mins

Serves 2-3

Ingredients

500g Courgette
Handful of fresh Mint leaves
200g cooked Lentils
Lemon Juice to taste

50g Feta Cheese
2 teaspoon Olive Oil
Lemon Zest
Salt and Pepper to taste

Preparation

✔ Using a potato peeler, slice the courgettes into long, wide slices.
✔ Mix with the oil and a pinch of salt.
✔ Heat a griddle pan until hot, then cook the courgette slices, turning once, until striped with grill stripes.
✔ Transfer the courgettes to a bowl and mix with the lemon zest, feta and lentils.
✔ Just before serving, mix through the ripped mint leaves.
✔ Add a little lemon juice and salt and pepper according to taste.

Serving Suggestion

This is a very light warm salad. If you feel like you need more, add some more lentils or serve with a chicken breast or a piece of fish.

Not Coleslaw –
Grated Carrot Side Salad!

Stay away from coleslaw. Coleslaw contains mayonnaise which is full of fat. Enjoy this as a healthy alternative.

Time in the Kitchen: 2 mins

Serve 1 carrot per/person

Ingredients

1 Carrot per person
Lemon Juice
A drizzle of Oil
Salt and Pepper to taste

Preparation

✔ Grate the carrot.
✔ Top with lemon juice, adjust according to taste.
✔ Drizzle with a little oil and season with salt and pepper.

Serving Suggestion

This is delicious in the summer with barbequed meat.

Cauliflower 'Rice'

I love this recipe; it is quick, easy and a great way of getting more vegetables onto your plate. Low-Carb, Slow Carb and is friendly to almost every diet out there. It also ticks all the boxes for Paleo, and Primal too. It's a great way of bulking up a dish, without bulking up the calories. Try it with a curry or a chilli con carne – once you get the sauce on it, you wouldn't even know you weren't eating rice. A large cauliflower goes a long way. Once you have prepared the 'rice', you can freeze it before cooking it and use it for future dishes.

Time in the Kitchen: 10–12 mins

Serves 2–3

Ingredients

1 head of Cauliflower

Preparation

- ✔ Before beginning, ensure the cauliflower is free from brown or black spots. If there are any visible, simply remove with a paring knife.
- ✔ Remove all the leaves from the bottom of the cauliflower and cut the cauliflower in half.
- ✔ Divide the cauliflower into florets until you are just left with the core.
- ✔ The core is full of goodness and you can use this too, however if you choose not to, simply discard it.
- ✔ Ensure all florets are broken up into relatively even sizes. Once this has been done, place the florets into a food processor and process until even chopped into 'rice' like pieces. Ensure you do not completely pulverize the cauliflower, apply a gentle setting and process at short intervals.
- ✔ Continue to do this, in small batches if necessary, until all the cauliflower has been processed. There are 2 ways in which you can now proceed...

Serving Suggestions

If you would prefer a drier 'rice', then I suggest you 'dry fry' the cauliflower in a frying pan so that would remove as much of the moisture as possible. Season with salt and pepper and even some spices which will suitably complement your dish.

An equally simple and effective way of cooking your rice is to steam it. This will give you a more moist texture. It does not need long at all in the steamer, 2-3 minutes will be plenty.

Once your rice is ready, you can then serve with a main dish of your choice.

Sweets and Desserts

Peanut Butter Bars

Sweet Potato Brownies

Banana and Blueberry Omelette

Gluten Free Banana Bread

Seeded Crunch

Pumpkin Seed Crunch

Toasted Almonds, Blueberries and Yoghurt

Warm Pineapple and Cinnamon

Peanut Butter Bars

This is a simple recipe for a really tasty treat. They can be used as a pre-workout pick-me-up or as a sweet treat. Go easy though, they are pretty calorie dense.

Time in the Kitchen: 10 mins

Serves 12

Ingredients

1 cup Sugar-free, Salt-free Peanut Butter
250ml Honey (local is best)
300g Oat Bran/Rolled Oats

Preparation

- ✔ Prepare a saucepan over a low heat.
- ✔ Place the peanut butter and honey into the saucepan and thoroughly combine until it becomes a liquid consistency.
- ✔ Keep stirring so ensure the mixture doesn't burn.
- ✔ Once you have achieved the liquid consistency, add the oat-bran/oats and mix well.
- ✔ Press the mixture onto a 20cm x 20cm baking sheet.
- ✔ Cover and let set overnight.
- ✔ Cut into 12–14 portions and serve.

Sweet Potato Brownies

Something different and a cheeky way of getting one of your 5-a-day!

Time in the Kitchen: 40 mins

Serves 16

Ingredients

100g Butter
150g of 70–85% Dark Chocolate, broken into pieces.
   (The more cocoa the better)
200g Sweet Potato, cooked and mashed
2 medium Eggs, beaten
2 teaspoon Vanilla Extract
125g Plain Flour
   (use gluten-free if preferred/required. You can also experiment with coconut, almond or rice flour to boost the guilt-free factor.)
½ teaspoon Baking Powder
50g Nuts (it is up to you which nuts you'd like to use, I opt for hazelnuts or almonds)

Preparation

✔ Preheat the oven to 180°C.
✔ Lightly grease a square 20cm cake tin with a little butter.
✔ Begin by melting your chocolate and butter.
✔ Do this slowly and gently over a very low heat or in the micro-wave.
✔ Once the chocolate has melted, combine it in a separate bowl with your sweet potato mash.
✔ Add the eggs and vanilla extract and beat until thick.
✔ Stir in the flour, baking powder and nuts and mix well.
✔ If the mixture is a little wet, add a little more flour.
✔ Pour the batter into the tin and bake for 20–25 minutes.
✔ Ensure the mix is firm to touch but slightly moist in the middle.
✔ Allow the brownies to cool before removing from the tin.

Serving Suggestion

Cut into squares and serve with ice cream or natural yoghurt and fresh fruit.

Banana and Blueberry Omelette

I absolutely love this for breakfast, or as a dessert. It is high in protein and contains natural sugars. The ideal guilt-free treat.

Time in the Kitchen: 10 mins

Serves 1

Ingredients

3 Eggs
1 medium Banana
3 tablespoons Blueberries
1 tablespoon Cinnamon (optional)
1 teaspoon Coconut Oil. Use butter if you do not have coconut oil

Preparation

✔ Preheat the grill to a medium to high heat.
✔ Cut the banana in half and then slice lengthways into 6-8 slices.
✔ In a small jug/bowl whisk the eggs and add the cinnamon and blueberries and set to one side.
✔ Meanwhile, melt the oil/butter in a frying pan over a medium heat.
✔ Lightly fry the banana for 2-3 minutes until soft.
✔ Pour the whisked eggs over the banana and fry for 3-5 minutes until the bottom of the omelette is cooked.
✔ Transfer the pan under the grill to finish off cooking the top of the omelette.
✔ Once all of the egg is cooked, transfer to a plate and serve.

Serving Suggestion

Add plain yoghurt and your choice of fresh berries.

Gluten Free Banana Bread

This is a great recipe for an on-the-go snack, a quick breakfast or something sweet for afters.

Time in the Kitchen: 50-60 mins

Serves 8-10

Ingredients

3 cups of Almond/Rice/Coconut/Buckwheat Flour
2 large ripe Bananas, mashed
¼ cup Coconut Oil
4 tablespoons Honey
1 teaspoon Vanilla Extract
1 teaspoon Baking Powder
1 teaspoon Cinnamon
¼ teaspoon Nutmeg
½ cup chopped Walnuts (optional)
¼ cup of Raisins (optional)

Preparation

✔ Preheat the oven to 180°C.
✔ Combine all the ingredients into a bowl and mix well.
✔ Ensure all the dry ingredients are well combined.
✔ Pour this batter into a greased mini loaf tin. Bake for 55 minutes until the loaf is cooked through.
✔ You can tell if the inside is cooked by slipping a small knife or skewer into the centre of the loaf, if it comes out clean, you can be sure the bread is cooked.

Seeded Crunch

This is a great snack or tasty treat. It's also delicious served with almond milk for breakfast – a good way to add diversity to the start of your day.

Time in the Kitchen: 25-35 mins

Serves 8-12

Ingredients

½ cup Raw Sunflower Seeds
½ cup Raw Pumpkin Seeds
1 cup Almond Meal
1 cup Shredded Unsweetened Coconut
2 cups Almonds chopped
½ cup Coconut Oil
½ cup Honey
1 tablespoon Vanilla Extract
2 tablespoons unsweetened Cacao Powder
Cinnamon to taste

Preparation

- ✔ Preheat oven to 160°C.
- ✔ In a large bowl, combine all the dry ingredients and mix well.
- ✔ Over a low heat in a small to medium sized saucepan, combine all the wet ingredients.
- ✔ Once warm, pour the wet ingredients over the dry seed and nut mixture and mix well until everything is coated.
- ✔ Evenly spread the mixture over a lined baking sheet – do not wash the bowl.
- ✔ Bake in the oven for 15 minutes.
- ✔ Remove from the oven and return the mixture to the mixing bowl.
- ✔ Mix it well. This will ensure that the mixture doesn't burn and will give it a slight coating from any moisture left in the bowl previously.
- ✔ Return the mixture to the baking sheet, spread it out evenly one more time and place back in the oven for a further 15 minutes.
- ✔ Remove and let it cool.
- ✔ The crunch tastes better cold and also develops its crunchiness as it cools.

Serving Suggestion

Serve in a bowl with some almond milk or coconut milk or eat on its own as a healthy snack/treat.

Pumpkin Seed Crunch

This recipe of great for keeping in the cupboard for when you fancy something a little sweet or perhaps you have guests popping over for tea. It can store in an air tight container for up to 5 days.

Time in the Kitchen: 15-25 mins

Serves 6-12

Ingredients

1 cup of Pumpkin Seeds
3 ½ tablespoons Honey
1½ teaspoon of Paprika
½ teaspoon Cayenne Pepper
Pinch of Salt

Preparation

✔ Preheat the oven to 180°C.
✔ Combine all the ingredients into a bowl and mix well.
✔ Spread the mixture over a baking sheet lined with parchment / baking paper and bake for 15-20 minutes or until lightly golden.
✔ Once completely cooled, break into bite-size portions.

Toasted Almonds, Blueberries and Yoghurt

I absolutely love the flavour which comes from toasting almonds. The toasted almond and blueberry flavours complement each other really well. This recipe just offers a simple twist to just the usual fruit and yoghurt.

Time in the Kitchen: 5-7 mins

Serves 1-2

Ingredients

100g Greek/Natural Yoghurt or Fromage Frais
3 tablespoons of Blueberries (frozen or fresh)
2 tablespoons Flaked Almonds
1 teaspoon Honey (optional)

Preparation

✔ Preheat a dry frying pan over a high heat until hot.
✔ Add the almonds and dry fry until golden brown.
✔ Keep an eye on the almonds as they can easily burn , ensure you are tossing/stirring them continuously.
✔ Once done combine the remaining ingredients in a bowl.
✔ Sprinkle with the toasted almonds, a drizzle of honey if desired.

Warm Pineapple and Cinnamon

I absolutely love this dish. It is so simple to make and the flavours work really well together. It is a great way to finish off a meal and is guilt-free too.

Time in the Kitchen: 10-15 mins

Serves 4

Ingredients

2 tablespoons clear Honey (local if possible)
1 teaspoon Cinnamon
2 teaspoon Butter
1 whole Pineapple, skinned, cored and cut into 8 long wedges
200g Fromage Frais (optional, to serve)

Preparation

✔ Heat the butter and honey in a non-stick frying pan until melted.
✔ Add the pineapple and fry until caramelised ensuring you are turning regularly.
✔ Just before the pineapple is fully cooked, sprinkle with cinnamon and fry for a further 1-2 minutes.

Serving Suggestions

Serve immediately alone or with a dollop of fromage frais.
For an added twist, flavour the fromage frais with a little cinnamon before serving.